EXPLORING THE WORLD OF
Owls

Tracy C. Read

FIREFLY BOOKS

A FIREFLY BOOK

Published by Firefly Books Ltd. 2011

First Printing

Publisher Cataloging-in-Publication Data
(U.S.)
Read, Tracy C.
    Exploring the world of owls /
Tracy C. Read.
[24] p. : col. photos. ;   cm.
Includes index.

ISBN-13: 978-1-55407-883-7 (bound)
ISBN-10: 1-55407-883-0 (bound)
ISBN-13: 978-1-55407-957-5 (pbk.)
ISBN-10: 1-55407-957-8 (pbk.)
1. Owls. I. Title.
598.97 dc22   QL696.S8R434   2011

Library and Archives Canada
    Cataloguing in Publication
Read, Tracy C.
    Exploring the world of owls /
Tracy C. Read.
Includes index.
ISBN-13: 978-1-55407-883-7 (bound)
ISBN-10: 1-55407-883-0 (bound)
ISBN-13: 978-1-55407-957-5 (pbk.)
ISBN-10: 1-55407-957-8 (pbk.)
1. Owls--Juvenile literature. I. Title.
QL696.S8R43 2011
j598.9'7   C2011-902339-3

Published in the United States by
Firefly Books (U.S.) Inc.
P.O. Box 1338, Ellicott Station
Buffalo, New York 14205

Published in Canada by
Firefly Books Ltd.
66 Leek Crescent
Richmond Hill, Ontario L4B 1H1

The Publisher gratefully acknowledges the financial support for our publishing program by the Government of Canada through the Canada Bock Fund as administered by the Department of Canadian Heritage.

Cover and interior design by
Janice McLean/Bookmakers Press Inc.

Printed in Canada

Front cover: Northern saw-whet owl
    © mlorenz/Shutterstock

Back cover: Barn owl © Kenneth Rush/
    Shutterstock

Back cover, inset, left: Burrowing owl
    © Luis César Tejo/Shutterstock

Back cover, inset, right top: Barred owl
    © mlorenz/Shutterstock

Back cover, inset, right bottom: Great horned
    owl © Alan Gleichman/Shutterstock

CONTENTS

OWLS DOWN UNDER
The yellow-eyed litlle burrowing owl makes its nest underground and hunts its prey by day or night.

MEET THE OWLS

Late one autumn night a few years ago, my brother stepped outside to look at the starry sky over our cottage. Glancing up, he was astonished to see a large snowy owl staring down at him from the branch of a tall red pine tree. Almost before he could register the owl's presence, it launched itself from its perch and veered off toward the open water, the sound of its huge flapping wings a haunting whisper in the quiet air.

The snowy owl is one of a handful of owls that hunt by day, so my brother may have roused it from a nighttime nap. If it has stopped off on our northern Ontario island again, none of us have been lucky enough to see it. But that unforgettable sighting is a powerful example of the mix of fear and awe with which humans have always greeted the owl, a bird that has lived on Earth for at least 60 million years.

Worldwide, there are roughly 200 owl species belonging to two families, the Tytonidae (barn and bay owls) and the Strigidae (true owls). North America is home to 19. Most dwell in forest habitats, while some live in the Arctic tundra and in wetlands, deserts and prairies. Many hunt at dawn and dusk or in the dark of night, but a few seek out prey in broad daylight. Some migrate to escape the northern winters, while others live in their territories yearlong.

Let's find out more about one of the world's most secretive birds.

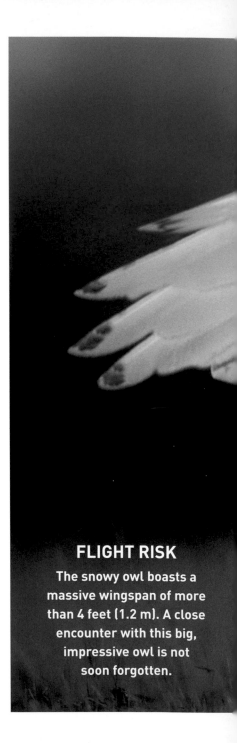

FLIGHT RISK

The snowy owl boasts a massive wingspan of more than 4 feet (1.2 m). A close encounter with this big, impressive owl is not soon forgotten.

ANATOMY LESSON

From the sparrow-sized elf owl to the thigh-high great gray, the owls that make their home in North America come in a remarkable range of sizes. But whether they're small, medium or large, all owls share hallmark traits that make them well suited to their lives as hunters.

Standing on its perch, the owl looks almost stocky. That's because its body is covered with feathers that are streamlined at the tip but fluffy and downy at the base. By trapping body heat, these specialized feathers help protect the owl from the cold and damp. In fact, the owl's feathers often grow right down to the tip of its toes, offering extra protection from the cold.

Its soft feathers and relaxed perching posture combine to make this bird's neck look rather short and stubby. However, the opposite is true. A long, flexible neck allows the owl to turn its head roughly 280 degrees, about 100 degrees more than a human can. This helps make up for the fact that the owl's big, tubular-shaped eyes take up so much head space, there's no room left for the muscles that would allow the owl to rotate its eyes in their sockets.

In some owl species — 9 out of 19 in North America and about

EARS TO YOU

The forest-dwelling long-eared owl has generous ear tufts, top, while the short-eared owl, center, a nomadic day hunter, boasts modest tufts. The great gray owl, bottom, has none.

ALL CREATURES GREAT AND SMALL

One of the smallest owls native to North America, the northern pygmy-owl is roughly 6 inches (15 cm) tall and weighs about 2½ ounces (71 g). It typically hunts at dusk and dawn. Its gray-brown feathers allow it to fade into the background as it flies from branch to branch on the lookout for small mammals or insects on the move.

40 percent worldwide — the classic owl head shape is disrupted by a feature called ear tufts. Not ears at all, these tufts are feathers that grow in a ridge on the top of the head and can be lifted and lowered by the owl. Researchers think that an owl uses its raised ear tufts to mimic the shape of a broken branch. While many of the owls that live in a forest setting have ear tufts, such as the great horned owl, the long-eared owl and the screech-owls, neither the boreal owl nor the great gray owl, both of which roost and hunt in woodland areas, has tufts.

The camouflaging color of an owl's body feathers, however, is the real reason this bird is able to hide in plain sight. The feathers of most owls are shades of gray, tan and brown, with spots, dashes and streaks that break up the color. During the day, a night-hunting owl can doze on a branch in the forest in relative peace, because it blends into its surroundings so perfectly. Similarly, the mostly white plumage of the snowy owl makes it hard to spot this raptor on the snow-covered tundra where it lives.

Depending on their habitat, some owl species may even appear in different hues, called morphs. The great horned owl living in the shady coastal rainforest, for exam-

ple, is much darker than its pale prairie-dwelling cousin. Many of the eastern screech-owls in humid Florida are reddish in color, while those in the dry west are more likely to be gray.

The owl's big eyes are set in the front of its head, like those of a human, and as a result, it looks at the world with an engaging yet intense stare. Its face is framed by a concave disk of feathers that conceals and protects its two ear openings. Bristle-like feathers cover its nostrils, shielding them from the cold.

The owl's facial feathers also disguise the size of its downward-curving beak, whose knife-sharp edges enable the owl to snap the neck of a small mammal in an instant. That can happen, of course, only after the prey has been snatched up in the raptor's strong, curved talons, which have been described as needle-sharp.

HOOKS & EYES

Owls have a third eyelid, known as a nictitating membrane, that clears away dust and debris from the surface of the eye. Above left, a great gray owl caught in midblink. The deadly talons of the great horned owl, above right, can grasp prey in a viselike grip.

Because it is a ferocious hunter, the great horned owl, seen here, earned its nickname "the flying tiger." At more than 3 pounds (1.4 kg), it's also one of the heaviest owls. Its typically long ear tufts are flattened here.

Weight range
In many species, the female is roughly one-fifth larger than the male. At about 4 pounds (1.8 kg), the snowy owl is the heaviest North American owl. The 1⅖-ounce (40 g) elf owl is the lightest.

'Rubberneck'
The owl has 14 vertebrae in its neck, while humans have 7.

Wing tips
The front edge of the leading wing feathers in many owls is fringed, which reduces the sound when an owl flaps its wings and glides.

Shake a tail feather
As an owl comes in for a landing, it spreads its tail feathers to slow down.

Feet
By shifting one of its three front toes to the back, the owl is able to widen its grasp. Rough soles supply a little extra traction to handle squirming prey.

Ear tufts
Part camouflage, part mood ring, the owl's ear tufts often indicate the owl's emotional outlook.

Eyes
An owl's oversized eyes are set in the front of its head. Shaped like tubes, rather than globes, the eyes cannot rotate in their sockets.

Light as a feather
Soft, fluffy body feathers make the owl look bigger than it actually is, an illusion that helps scare away predators.

Talons
These weapons are licensed to kill.

Height range
North America's tallest owl is the great gray, at about 27 inches (68 cm). The tiniest is the 6-inch (15 cm) elf owl.

WHERE'S WALDO?
The color and textured pattern of the owl's feathers help it fade into the background, as shown by these forest-loving owls: the yellow-eyed western screech-owl, left, the dark-eyed flammulated owl, below, and the barred owl, bottom.

NATURAL TALENTS

Like all birds of prey, owls depend on keen eyesight and above-average hearing to detect and capture their quick-moving quarry. But owls face an added challenge. Most species hunt at dusk and dawn or during the night, navigating dark, treacherous corridors of tree trunks and branches, snatching up meals and somehow finding their way back to their nests. How do they do it?

First, the owl's remarkably large eyes are specially built to see in low-light conditions and to adapt quickly as those conditions change. After all, early-evening light is very different from the light at midnight, a moonless night very different from one with a full moon.

An owl's pupils are designed to open wide to let in the maximum amount of light — almost three times more than a human pupil allows. This light strikes the retina, a thin layer at the back of the eye that is packed with rod cells, which respond to dim light and shades of black and white. In turn, the retina is connected to the brain by the optic nerve, which delivers messages to an owl's brain at lightning speed.

Present in lesser numbers are cone cells, which respond to color and bright light and are necessary for seeing well by day.

The owl's forward-looking eyes enable binocular vision, so it can judge distances and depths. Seeing the world in three dimen-

NIGHT OWL

Notable for its heart-shaped face and pale color, the medium-sized barn owl is one of four North American owls whose eyes are dark rather than yellow. Eye color, however, makes no difference in an owl's ability to see. This night-active owl lives all over the world, preferring open landscapes, and is the only representative of the barn owl family, Tytonidae, on this continent.

IN THE CROSSHAIRS

Braking by spreading its wing and tail feathers, its feet braced for contact, this northern pygmy-owl has locked its eyes on dinner and is moving in for the kill. Just before plucking up its prey, the owl closes its eyes for protection.

sions is an essential skill for a bird that has to focus on a moving target, such as a vole scurrying through tall grass. Capable of turning its head roughly 140 degrees in each direction, the owl can easily investigate sounds and sudden movements all around it.

An owl also enjoys a number of hearing advantages. Its feathered facial disk works like a satellite dish, gathering and directing sound waves to its ears. The ears of half the owl species in North America (usually night hunters) are positioned at different heights on either side of the owl's wide head. By turning and dipping its head, the owl can hear a sound in both ears at once and pinpoint its location. Then, the hunt is on.

The owl's undeveloped sense of smell doesn't play a role in prey capture, and its sense of taste and touch are not much better. But the owl does engage in regular mutual preening sessions with its mate and offspring, establishing family ties and keeping its feathers in top-flight condition.

SIGHT
Sensitive to dim lighting, an owl's very large eyes quickly detect and telegraph movement to the brain.

HEARING
With its fine-tuned hearing, an owl picks up vocalizations of other owls and the sounds of prey and predators.

SMELL
The owl's modest sense of smell does not play a role in its search for a meal.

TASTE
Skunk anyone? The owl's poor sense of taste means foul-flavored prey is not a problem.

TOUCH
The owl takes care of its feathers and those of its mate and owlets by preening with its beak.

HUNTING OWL-STYLE

In North America, owl species occupy almost every kind of habitat, from the frigid Far North and the continent's temperate center to steamy Florida and the southwestern deserts. No matter where the hot-blooded owl lives, however, it needs a constant source of calories to stay healthy and active. How does it fuel up?

While most owls are satisfied with a meal of small rodents, these birds have wide-ranging tastes that can include tiny flying insects and long wriggling snakes. Predictably, the heavier, stronger owls tackle larger prey, such as pheasants and jackrabbits, while the medium-sized barn owl regards a hefty Norway rat as fair game.

For all animals, the best way

to save energy is not to spend it in the first place. That's why the wise owl's preferred hunting strategy, especially when prey is scarce, is simply to sit and wait. From a perch where it can quietly watch and listen, an owl is able to quickly detect the most subtle movement or sound on the ground below.

Owls that depend primarily on their sharp vision, such as the snowy owl and the northern hawk owl, pick a tall roost where they can survey their territory from on high. Owls that rely more on sound to alert them to prey, such as the boreal and northern saw-whet, launch their attacks from perches closer to the action.

Sometimes described as the

SILENT, BUT DEADLY

Feathers at the front edge of the wings of many owls, including the great gray, great horned and snowy owls, have an uneven edge that breaks up and deadens the whooshing sound of air over the wings. A quiet, stealthy approach provides a distinct advantage over prey.

OWLISH TAKEDOWN

Even experienced hunters aren't always as lucky as this female snowy owl, which has nabbed a plump gray partridge. Only about one in three owl hunting expeditions is successful. To get through a dry patch, a snowy owl can survive a near-starvation diet until the hunting improves.

BIG GULP
Swallowing one of its favorite little mammals whole, a barred owl makes quick work of a flying squirrel.

IT'S NOT WHAT YOU THINK
Owls cough up the indigestible parts of their prey in the form of cigar-shaped pellets. By dissecting this snowy owl pellet, wildlife writer/photographer Wayne Lynch identified lemming bones and fur and a single bird beak.

nighttime equivalent of eagles and hawks, the carnivorous owls are considered raptors — birds that secure their meals by seizing small animals with their feet and beaks. Indeed, as the owl approaches its target from the air, it spreads its wing and tail feathers to slow down, thrusting its feet forward and straightening its legs in one motion. That movement causes its toes to spread, and when it makes contact, its legs bend and its talons close around the prey, often fatally puncturing it. If that doesn't do the trick, the owl finishes the animal off with its razor-edged beak, which it also uses to slice and dice prey into bite-sized pieces for its young.

Some owls hunt using a low-level flying style known as coursing. Flapping their wings and gliding slowly and silently back and forth over open ground, the short-eared, long-eared and barn owls watch for the slightest movement. Smaller, quicker owls, such as the flammulated owl and the elf owl, catch their dinner on the fly, snatching insects out of thin air with their talons, in a technique called hawking.

Sometimes, it just makes sense to chase down dinner on the ground. The long-legged burrowing owl captures insect meals by trapping them underfoot, and even the great gray owl has been seen marching after prey as it attempts to flee into the bush.

The owl kills its prey quickly, either by swallowing it or carrying it off to a secure roost where it can dine in peace, far from the greedy eyes of larger, fiercer predators.

HYBRID HUNTER

The slender body, pointed wings and long tail may be hawklike, but there's no mistaking the round owl head of the medium-sized northern hawk owl. This raptor lives in the boreal forest, hunting by day in open areas. After eating its fill, it may cache, or hide, extra treats for later.

WHAT'S ON THE OWL'S MENU?

Many owls specialize in small mammals, such as voles, mice, shrews and pocket gophers. Larger owls prey on rabbits, snowshoe hares and waterfowl. But songbirds, crayfish, frogs, lizards, snakes, beetles and other insects will do too.

OWL FAMILY DYNAMIC

Owls kick off the mating season a little earlier than most birds. Long before the snow melts, increasing minutes of daylight trigger the owls' sex hormones, and soon, the forest explodes with the sound and sight of the owls' courtship rituals.

The female owl has the final say in mate selection, and the male isn't shy about proving his worth. Through vigorous vocalizations, dazzling flying displays and gifts of food, the male shows off his health, strength and survival skills. The male short-eared owl, for example, launches himself into the air, then dramatically dives toward the ground, clapping his wings as he hurtles downward. After as many as a dozen of these energy-sapping performances, he finally settles next to the female, as if waiting to hear how he scored.

Once the female chooses her mate, the male and female go house hunting. Harshly speaking, owls are squatters, preferring to move into preexisting digs that don't demand much from the new tenants. The smallest owls — the elf, the flammulated and the northern saw-whet — may take over the abandoned nest holes of a woodpecker. The great gray is content to call a broken tree trunk home, the barn owl likes to inhabit old buildings or cliffside caves, and the snowy owl and the short-eared owl both nest on the ground. As per its name, the bur-

POWER FAMILY

Tall and heavy, with a 5-foot (1.5 m) wingspan, the great horned owl is the most successful owl in North America. It hunts some 250 prey items, adapting easily to what's on the local menu. Its two to four chicks rely on their parents for food long after they've left the nest.

rowing owl sets up housekeeping underground, in the deserted burrow of a prairie dog, badger or coyote. In regions where the soil is soft, it digs its own tunnel.

After laying her eggs, the female keeps her clutch warm via a featherless section of skin on her belly called a brood patch. There may be two eggs or as many as 13, depending on the species and the availability of food. The little elf owl incubates her eggs for 24 days, while the snowy may spend up to 33 days on the nest, taking the occasional bathroom break. It's a long haul for the mother, whose only real source of entertainment is gently turning the eggs four or five times a day with her beak. The silver lining? Even before the eggs are laid, most

SNACK-MEISTER

Her chicks may have left home, but for another two months, the burrowing owl mother serves up meals as the youngsters fine-tune their hunting skills.

male owls deliver dinner to the mother, stockpiling it in the nest if the hunting is good.

Covered with whitish down, the chicks break out of their egg prison using a hard pointed tip on their beak called an egg tooth. Their eyes open in about 10 days.

The male's responsibilities as breadwinner now multiply, with hungry, demanding owlets to feed. The smaller owl species are ready to fly in about four weeks, while the larger owls take 9 to 10 weeks. Many exit the nest before learning to fly, perhaps to escape

a dirty, crowded environment.

Once the chicks are airborne, though, life's tough lessons begin. Eventually, their pleas for food are ignored by parents urging them to become independent. After a few more weeks of skills training, adult life is bumpily under way.

ALL IN THE FAMILY

The female owl starts to incubate each egg shortly after it is laid. These boreal owlets are slightly different sizes because they hatched days apart. So far, each seems to have survived the sibling food fight that is part of early owl life.

THE GOONIES

This great gray owlet will grow up to be one of the world's most recognizable owls, but for now, it's just a funny-looking chick.

PHOTOS © TIM FITZHARRIS

p. 4-5

p. 6 top

p. 11 top

PHOTOS © WAYNE LYNCH

p. 6 middle

p. 8 right

p. 9 both photos

p. 11 middle

p. 14

p. 16 both

p. 17

p. 18 both

p. 19 top

p. 20 bottom

p. 22-23 all photos

PHOTOS © SHUTTERSTOCK

p. 3 Rusty Dodson

p. 6 bottom: Stephen Mcsweeney

p. 7 Ronnie Howard

p. 8 Pics-xL

p. 10 Eric Isselée

p. 11 bottom: artcphotos

p. 13 mlorenz

p. 15 mlorenz

p. 19 rabbit: nialat

p. 19 frog: Jason Patrick Ross

p. 19 duck: Evgeniya Uvarova

p. 19 bird: Paul Binet

p. 20 top: Colette3

p. 21 Ronnie Howard